COSELEY

A Walk Back in Tim

To Iris

Best wishes
always

Beryl

Front cover: The canal at Ivyhouse Lane, Coseley

Back cover: The Headquarters of The Tipton and Coseley
Building Society at Owen Street, Tipton

COSELEY
A walk back in time

by C. Beryl Wilkes

BREWIN BOOKS

First published in 1983 by
Brewin Books, Studley, Warwickshire, B80 7LG

New Revised Edition December 1994

© C. Beryl Wilkes 1983 & 1994

All rights reserved

ISBN 1 85858 046 3

Made and printed in Great Britain by
Supaprint (Redditch) Ltd.

Dedicated
to the blessed memory of my parents
Wallace and Emily Hyde

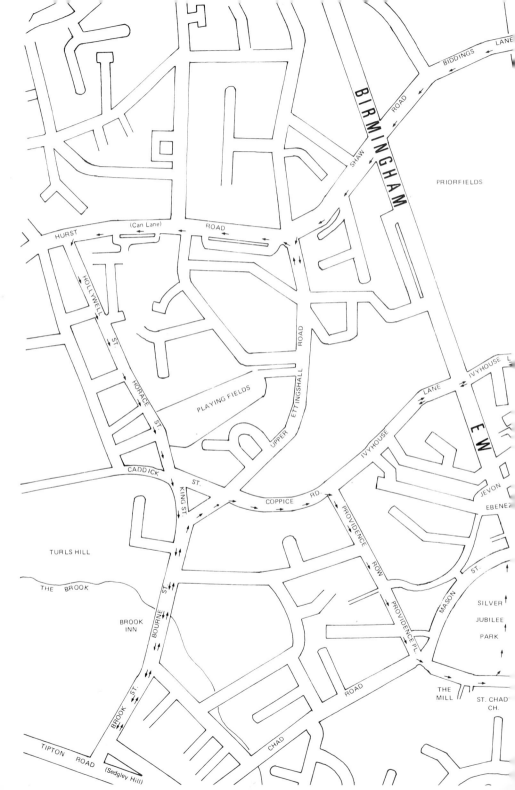

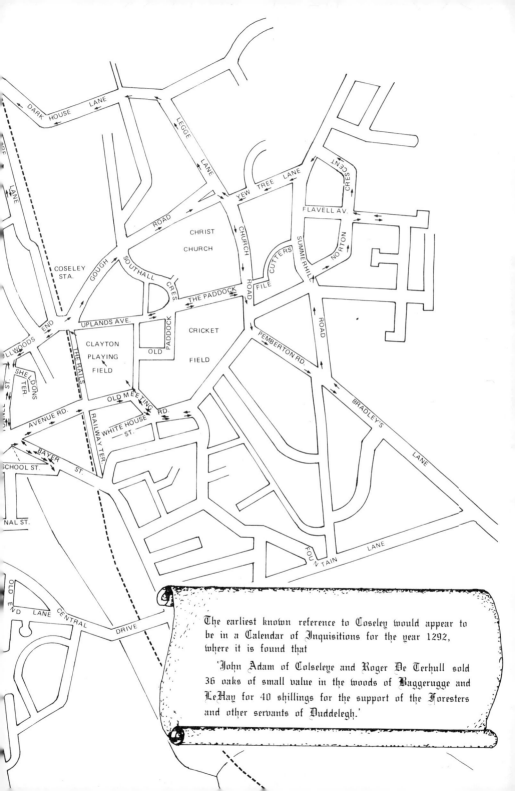

The earliest known reference to Coseley would appear to be in a Calendar of Inquisitions for the year 1292, where it is found that

'John Adam of Colseleye and Roger De Terhull sold 36 oaks of small value in the woods of Baggerugge and LeHay for 40 shillings for the support of the Foresters and other servants of Duddelegh.'

Wednesday, 8th November, 1933 at 3.00 p.m.

The opening of the Coseley Branch of the Tipton & Coseley Building Society, Roseville House, The Square, Coseley, Councillor J.A. Grange, J.P. (centre) who performed the opening ceremony.

Mr. J.C. Roper (Clerk to Coseley Council), Mr. E.H. Hipkins (Chairman of the Tipton & Coseley Building Society), Councillor J.A. Grange (Chairman of Coseley Council) and Mr. Walter Jeavons standing behind Mr. D.H. Hartland (Secretary of the T & C Building Society).

The Airedale was never far away from his master, Councillor Grange. His Kennel Club name was Ahmley Crusader but was know to all as Paddy.

TIPTON & COSELEY BUILDING SOCIETY

The Tipton Building Society was founded in 1901. Its first Secretary was Percy J.W. Brown who held this position until 1905. The first Chairman of Directors was Oliver Howl until 1903.

Business was first conducted in the Owen Street office of Charles Round, Solicitor, which practice later joined with Stockdale & Brown and moved to High Street, close to the canal bridge, and the Society with it. The old houses that comprised these offices were purchased and demolished in 1962 and new offices erected on the site were opened in June 1963. These in turn were sold in 1993 when the Society moved to imposing purpose built offices in Owen Street.

Early in the century Mr. D.H. Hartland, a clerk on the Staff of Stockdale & Brown became Secretary to the Society and remained in that capacity until his death in 1949. Arnold Sowden who had been joint Secretary with Mr. Hartland then took over until his retirement in 1958.

Mr. Stuart Eaton, was then appointed by the Directors to follow Mr. Sowden. He had been on the Staff since leaving Dudley Grammar School at the age 14. The present Chief Executive, Mr. Christopher Martin joined the Society straight from school too, when in 1970 he left Tipton Grammar School.

Contributions were taken at Coseley before 1932 but in 1993 a Branch Office of what was then called Tipton & District Permanent Benefit Building Society was officially opened in Roseville by the then Chairman of Coseley Urban District Council, Cllr. J.A. Grange, J.P. (Incidentally the son of the Chairman of the Council married the daughter of the Secretary of the Building Society in 1935). The name was subsequently changed to Tipton and Coseley Building Society.

Branches are now open in Dudley, Sedgley and Bilston.

The Society is now fully computerised in contrast to the early days when all was done by hand and a thorough knowledge of arithmerical tables and processes, particularly, simple interest and percentages was required.

The names of depositors and borrowers were annually written by hand in a large ledger and each contributor had a personal book.

Similarly what borrowers still owed was calculated and inserted in the book by aid of pen and ink.

Interest to be paid to investors was calculated by the Secretary and his assistants and cheques sent out on June 30th and December 31st.

The Secretary often worked on Boxing Day and was even known to work on a Christmas Day.

Now, however, the Society has continued to prosper and maintain its independence while others have amalgamated. Great credit is due to able and enterprising Directors and Management over these years in supplying a need for the immediate districts. The present Chairman is R. Derek Buxton who took the Chair in February 1993.

May the Society continue to prosper.

FOREWORD

This book by Beryl Wilkes is the sequel to her first book "A walk back in time around Coseley" which was a photographic record and descriptions of the inhabitants and buildings seen in a walk around the old Coseley.

This was a most nostalgic look at a Coseley almost lost, with not many traces today. It was a time of large open spaces with small centres of population.

In this her second book Beryl Wilkes repeated the walk over the same route many years later. It is another look at this once Great Urban District of Coseley (being one of the largest in England.) She notes the changes that have taken place, buildings and streets disappearing and many people not missing them.

This book is written by someone who has a love for Coseley, having lived there all her life.

A good read for all and Coseley people in particular.

DOUG BAKER

INTRODUCTION

This new and completely revised edition has been written following the interest gererated by the first edition in 1983. It was originally intended to reprint the first edition in full, with an appendix, but much has happened in Coseley and new photographs have come to light. Printing technology too has moved on and I have taken advantage of our printer's new facilities to print the cover photograph in colour and the remaining photographs by a new and improved method.

So many additional photographs have come to light, it has been decided to hold over most of the additional photographs for use in a further book for publication in the Autumn of 1995.

C. Beryl Wilkes
November 1994.

Since my companion and I walked a-round Coseley in 1983 several changes have taken place. If you would like to walk around Coseley we'll go together but first I must tell you why we are starting from 2, Central Drive. It's the house where I grew up but the address then was 50 Old End Lane. In fact the first four houses in Central Drive were all in Old End Lane but they were re-numbered and included in Central Drive when that road was cut through right into Fountain Lane in the late 1950's.

From here in the garden we could see Jack Nicholl's builders yard, the field where Guest's the butchers grazed their cows and beyond that, over the other side of the canal, the houses in Wall-brook.

The Apple Tree pub was opened in September 1961. The licencee then was Bill Nicholls who moved from the old Apple Tree pub in Castle Street to the imposing new building which stands where the builders yard and Guests field used to be.

1.

Taken in the garden of 50 Old End Lane with Mr. Nicholl's builders yard in the background and some houses in Wallbrook in the distance in 1936.

The Apple Tree Inn, 1994

2.

1

From here we can see the Trustees Savings Bank and Midital, a shop which sells fireplaces and decorative plaster accessories.

3.   Midital and the Trustees Savings Bank

Before this building was here there was a beautiful cinema called the Clifton. It was built during 1938 and '39 and it closed in 1963. Before the Clifton occupied the space there was a large house there, but we must get on. We've several miles to go.

There has been a big change here. Now there is an island and Green Street has been cut through not only to the top of Central Drive but into The Square as well which makes Castle Street much safer for pedestrians although it is still used by buses and some lighter traffic. It was officially opened on the 23rd. August 1989 at 11 a.m. by Cllr. J.J. Curley of Dudley Highways Department who was accompanied by Cllr. Pauline Richards, Cllr. G.H. Davies and Cllr. J.T. Wilson at which time trees were planted to mark the occasion.

4.   Mrs. Kath York (extreme right) looking on approvingly. Kath was born 7th. December, 1922 and died on 22nd. November, 1993.

5.   Tree planting at the opening of Green Street by-pass 23rd. August, 1989.

We'll start by crossing over the top of Central Drive and the end of Green Street by-pass and walk towards the bus stop in Castle Street. This is where there used to be three large terraced houses one of which was lived in by Mr. Nicholls whose builders yard was just beyond his back garden. After the houses there was a drive before a shop which was kept by Mrs. Ethel Poutney when Mrs. Round gave up the business. She sold bread, cakes and confectionary. Joined to the side of the shop were two houses with an entry between them. Before the war there was a cottage next which lay back from the footpath. Mr. William Morgan, better known as "Smiler" used to live there. The cottage which was very old was demolished about the time of the beginning of the second world war. In it's place was put a huge round tank to conserve water to put out fires caused by enemy bombs, should there be any.

After this was a high wall which ran to the corner of Canal Street. No longer does Canal Street look as it did when Mrs. Fletcher lived there. It has been blocked off to allow for Green Street by-pass.

6.

Canal Street on 5th. October, 1994.

There are now car parks on both sides of Canal Street where houses used to stand. Wardell's 'pop' factory was the last building in Green Street to be demolished, that was about 1988, and we used to be able to see it from here. Someone who remembers Canal Street as it was is Bill Millard who, although no longer a resident of Coseley, visits relatives and friends from time to time.

7.

Mr. William (Bill) Millard
10th. May, 1993

3

Turn around and walk back towards Castle Street.
Now we can see Coseley Post Office and next to it is Guest's butchers shop then an optician and a dentist. It's along there where Mrs. Charlotte Morgan and Mrs Emma Price had their shops. There was an entry between their shops in about the same place as the wide passage is now. That leads to a car park we shall see later.

8.
Coseley Post Office and Guest's butchers shop.

The Post Office used to be in The Square and Mr. Guest's was just up here on this side of the road. Here on the corner is the freezer centre called Butcher Boy. This is exactly where the Apple Tree pub used to be. Next to it was Hyde's sweet shop. It used to be a ladies hat shop that is why it said M.I. HYDE Draper & Milliner above the window. After that there were about three terraced houses. The front doors opened onto the footpath, then there was a shop which I remember was a cobblers at one time. It had living premises between the cobblers shop and the chemists shop. The chemist was Mr. Marsh Fellows. His shop was attached to the living quarters of the shop next door. This was the one that was Guest's the butchers.

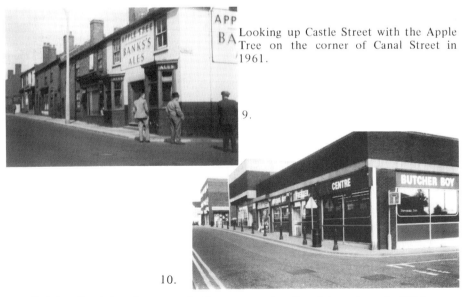

Looking up Castle Street with the Apple Tree on the corner of Canal Street in 1961.

9.

10.
Butcher Boy taken from exactly the same spot as the picture above in 1994.

At the back of the shop were the cow sheds. It is difficult to imagine that the cows were driven down to the field and then back again to be milked on these premises. Guest's milkman was named Sid Meese and he used to come around with a horse drawn cart. The milk churns had different sized containers hanging around the inside of them - 1 pint, ½ pint, 1 gill - and the milk would be poured into the customers own jug.

11. The cow sheds at the back of ....the shop. 12.

This was all where Prima haberdashery is and Lo-Cost was until November 1994 when it closed and was re-opened by Late Shopper.

One day I met Bill Rowley here.

13.

Mr. William (Bill) Rowley

Next in Castle Street was Nicklin's greengrocers and that was next to Joseph Smith's grocers shop. It was a real family business. Mrs. Smith also served in the shop as well as their sons Gilbert and Neville along with their wives Ivy and Mary. Between this shop and the next was a passage called Rabbit Row where there were several small houses. The Boddison family lived in one. There were two brothers: Albert was small, only about 3feet tall and Walter who was over 6 feet in height. Amazing! The next shop in Castle Street on the corner of Rabbit Row was Udall's butchers. They had two shops in the village and this one was managed by Bill Reynolds. He died in 1962 when he was 53. Next was a fish and chip shop, up two or three steps from the footpath. Mrs. Whitehouse kept this shop. All of these were where the video shop, the Tipton & Coseley Building Society, the hairdressers and the general store/off-licence is now.
Where Roseville Court is there were three shops with living accommodation: Mrs. Horton's shoe shop, Mrs. Morgan's fish and chip shop and Mrs. Tunley's sweet shop which was built onto the side of the White Lion, and that is still here.

The three shops which occupied the space
now the car park in Roseville Court next
to which can be seen the White Lion pub.

14.

15. The White Lion as it is today taken from the same spot as the picture above.

On the other side of the White Lion was Horton's butchers then Parkes's chemist. Over
sixty years ago the chemist was Mr. Toy. He sold the business to Mr. L.W. Parkes in
1933. Mr. Bullock went to the shop in 1965 and he took over from Mr. Parkes in
1967. More about this when we cross the road shortly. Next, there was a gated drive
and the last building, which stood on the corner of School Street, was Udall's other
butchers shop where George Udall used to work. What was the chemist's was re-built
in very similar style is now a pet shop on the ground floor and a hairdressers above.
There is a rest area where the butchers shop was.

Corner of School Street showing George
Udall's butcher's shop and Mr. Bullock's
chemist.

16.

The rest area on the
corner of School
Street where George
Udall's used to be.

17.

Davies's cake shop (left) and
what had been Fellows's hardware
after both businesses had
ceased trading.
This building looked directly
down School Street.

18.

We are going to walk back on the other side of the road so we'll cross over here. We are now on the corner where Jevon Street meets Castle Street. This is where Mr. & Mrs. Leonard Fellows had their hardware shop.

19.

Mr. Len Fellows with his son Roger on the step of the shop.

20.

Mrs. Irene Fellows. This picture shows Mr. Fullard's house on the corner of Jevon Street with Bank Street.

Next to it was Tommy Davies's cake shop then the long, one storey building that was the bake house.

This later became the Gas Board Showroom and subsequently Clarke's Radio before it was demolished to make way for a superior chemist's shop to where Mr. Bullock moved from across the road.

21.

22.

Mr. Bullock has been here since June 1985 about the same time that he went into partnership with Mr. Millard. Next door to them is a mini-market and off-licence called Save and Save.

On the waste land next to Save and Save used to be a wool shop owned by Mrs. Ida Rowberry and later by Mrs. Dorothy Bradley. Next to it was a green-grocers which before then was a cobbler's shop owned by Mr. Horton whose wife had the shoe shop across the road. Next were two houses up some steps and behind them two more houses. Some people named Fones lived in one of them. Next to the houses was a paint and wallpaper shop owned by Mr. Greenshill then there was George Mason's, the grocer's: just one in a nation-wide chain of shops. There were two George Mason's in Roseville. I'll show you the other one soon. After Mason's sold the shop there were several other businesses carried on here the last being a haberdashery called Yungeland. The name was changed to Prima when they moved over the road. We saw that on our way up the street. The next shop was Rapairwell Dry Cleaners. There was a wide entry between this and the next shop which had been Darby's wet fish shop for years. It had been Sam Darby's long before it became his son Eric's although he had worked there along side his mother and father. Eric's wife Mary also worked in the shop at times. Next to this was the Royal Hotel. The Royal Hotel is still there but Eric's fish shop has gone. The building just collapsed late on the evening of Tuesday, 18th February, 1986. A very sad day for Mr. & Mrs. Darby.

23.

Eric Darby on the shop steps of 55, Castle Street in 1981.

Although there is a mobile fish monger who visits Roseville on Tuesday's and Friday's Eric is still very much missed. It was at this time that the Royal Hotel was extended.

The shops alongside Eric Darby's, Repairwell and Yungeland, were shored up, but for the sake of safety very soon ceased trading and within a short while were demolished.

Eric and Mrs. Eileen Guest from the butchers shop were brother and sister. Eric died in May 1989.

24.

The morning after the shop collapsed Wednesday, 19th February, 1986.

Here we are now outside the Royal Hotel. It is about 30 years since the steps were taken away from the end of the building where it meets the bottom of Ebenezer Street. The steps led up to the door of Barclays Bank. Yes they did! Where the window is now on the corner is where the door was. Years before this within the same building but just up Ebenezer Street there was a shop which was a corn merchants belonging to Mr. Jordon. He moved to The Square and I'll show you soon where the Bank premises were moved to.

25.

The Royal Hotel.

Turn right up Ebenezer Street. Look left down Groucutt Street. The Relieving Office is missing. About five years ago this was another building which fell down. Here on the left is the car park reached by the passage in Castle Street. On the corner of Ebenezer Street and Groucutt Street there used to be a pub called "The Bush".

26.

The Relieving Office in 1981.

27.

Groucutt Street today minus the Relieving Office.

Here on the right in Ebenezer Street where there used to be some terraced houses and the house called "Roseleigh" which belonged to Horace Smout, the local coal merchant, and the coal yard stood is now Jack Newell Court. We can only see the side of the building from here.

28.

The south side of Jack Newell Court built in 1988 and
Ebenezer Baptist Chapel built in 1857.

The gully which used to link Ebenezer Street with Jevon Street is no longer there as it was built over during the alterations, so we must walk up the New Road. Before we do just look at these two shops on our left. The first belongs to Mr. Gordon Allen and his wife. They run a first class shoe repairers and new shoe shop. This is where they moved to in 1979 when they gave up the little shop in Fullwoods End. This shop here belonged to Mrs. Allen (no relation) who was the mother of Mrs. Edna Spicer who, with her husband Claude, ran a sweet and tobacconist business in the next shop. Later they also traded in china and glass. When they retired the shop was bought by Mr. Anthony Sturgess who deals in televisions and beautiful table and standard lamps and light fittings.

If we walk up to the corner and turn around we will see it much better.

Sturgess's shop (right) and Allen's shoe shop.   29.

I remember meeting my
Auntie here some years
ago.
She died on 11th February,
1992.

30.

Mrs. Victoria A. Hyde
near Ebenezer Baptist Chapel.

We'll walk now to the brow of the hill. If you'd seen this place before you'd now ask, "Where is the top of Jevon Street and Jeavons's shop and bakery and South Street where there were some houses and Arthur Davies's bicycle shop? I'll tell you where they are! Under Jack Newell Court.

31.

South Street with Roseville
in the background

32.

The shop at the top of Jevon Street
which years ago was Jeavons's.
The last owners were Walton Brothers.

Walton Brothers dealt in television hire and rental. The business was transferred from 18 Jevon Street to 647 Birmingham New Road, one of the shops just beyond Barclays Bank, in 1986. Mr. Malcolm (Mac) Walton died on 30th November, 1989. The shop is still empty and not only that - the Bank has been closed.

We'll turn right into Bank Street where the redundant Barclays Bank is over on the opposite corner, right again just where the Air Raid Post and the British Legion used to be and we'll see the front of Jack Newell Court.
One of the most well known people in Coseley lives here. Of course I mean Len Millard who was Captain of West Bromwich Albion Football team when they won the F.A. Cup in 1954. He left the Albion in 1956.

33.

Len Millard
16th July, 1994.

34.

Dudley Metropolitan Housing Services Committee
JACK NEWELL COURT, 11th July 1988

This sheltered housing scheme is dedicated to the memory of the late Councillor Jack Newell in recognition of his work with the elderly and disabled.

Now you can see what happened to the top of Jevon Street. About half of it is left and we'll go down it into Castle Street.

We are now back on the corner where Jevon Street joins Castle Street where Mr. & Mrs. Fellows had their shop. Before we go into The Square let's just go down School Street past where the side of George Udall's shop was and the little houses and we can have a good look at Green Street by-pass.

35.

School Street as it used to be with the
Council House centre of picture.

36.

Green Street looking south.

37.

Green Street looking north.

Back up School Street now and turn right into Castle Street towards The Square. Over the road on the corner of Bank Street with Castle Street there used to be a shop with the door situated across the corner. This was the other George Mason's that I told you about earlier on. We used to call this shop 'corner Mason's'. It had a window in both streets. It all looks so different now from how it used to be with the houses on the right and the shops on the left and the Post Office in the building that curved round Tunnel Street into Avenue Road. There is a car park where the houses used to be.

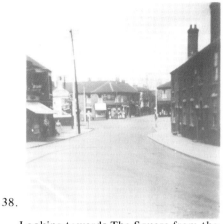

38.

Looking towards The Square from the corner of Jevon Street in the 1950's.

39.

Roseville Square in the 1960's.

40.

Roseville Square, 1994.

14

The Red Lion, which when built not long before the last war, replaced an old pub know as The Chain Yard, has been re-named The Old Chain Yard.
Many people have always called the Red Lion "The Chain Yard". So what's new?

41.

The Old Chain Yard

One day here I met old friends and neighbours Margery Humphrey and Louie Rhodes.
Mrs. Rhodes died October 1993.

42.

Mrs. Margery Humphrey (nee Turner) and Mrs. Louisa Rhodes (nee Mason).

Cross over the end of Green Street by-pass. This is exactly where the large house called "Roseville House" used to stand. Turn right into Bayer Street. Roseville Methodist Chapel is on our right but we can't see it very well from here because the trees have grown so much, so we'll look at it from the other side after we've turned the corner where Albert Grainger's cobblers shop used to be. On the right where my first home, 17 Bayer Street, used to be is a single storey building: the Social Services Office of Dudley Metropolitan Borough which was officially opened on Monday, 29th September, 1986. Over on the left, the building which was Mr. Hingley's shop and home, is the Rent Office which also belongs to Dudley Metropolitan Borough.

15

43.

The houses which stood where the Social Services Offices are today
in Bayer Street.

44.

The houses which were demolished and the building which today is
the Rent Office in Bayer Street.

45.

Bayer Street Clinic was officially opened on 4th December, 1937 by
Cllr. Samuel Davies, J.P., F.F.I.

Next to the Rent Office is the Clinic which was smartened up and given a new roof in 1989. In the same grounds as the Clinic is a two storey building where Coseley 1st Cubs and Scouts meet. They are kept well 'in line' by Scout Master Ron Darby and 'Akela' who is Ron's wife Madeline. A few years ago Mrs. Darby had a Scout award for Meritorious Conduct since when she has had a long service award. I've been reliably informed that the Scout premises were scheduled to be a decontamination centre in the event of a gas attack during the war.

46. The Scout premises, Bayer Street.   47.   Ron and Madeline Darby
                                               ('Skip' and 'Akela')

Now we'll turn right into School Street. Behind the fence on the left is "Bridge House", one of the Homes belonging to Dudley Metropolitan Borough.
There used to be a nice big house in those grounds called "The Warren". It was demolished in 1981. The Charnell family lived there.

48.   49.

Sunlight on "The Warren" shortly   A group of children photographed
before it's demolition in 1981.   in the grounds of "The Warren"
                                          August, 1933.

17

Walk on the footpath and bear right around the corner. This is where Len Barnett had a big brick built garage where he kept his char-a-bancs (coaches). He used to take people on trips and in 1928 he took a party of ladies to the Midland Counties Dairy in Birmingham. They had their photograph taken and Mrs. Barnett (not Len's wife) sat on the front row with her little baby Alan.

50.

Coseley ladies and children on the outing to
Midland Counties Dairy, Birmingham in 1928.

Alan Barnett, the smallest baby on the above group lived in School Street. He grew up to be an extremely adept and well known Snooker player. So good was he that in 1961 he won the All England Amateur Snooker Championship.

51.

Alan Barnett - born 26th January, 1928, died 2nd October, 1991.

18

Opposite Len Barnett's garage was a pub called the Summer House.
The grounds at the back of it were fascinating as they took the form of a maze or puzzle garden: quite unique in Coseley. The pub was still there in 1960. Sometime later there was a large wooden hut there. It was used as a meeting centre for Senior Citizens and when needed, as a Polling Station.
I'll tell you more about it later on.

52.

The hut which stood where the Summer House used to be in School Street.

Since Green Street has been extended into The Square it has cut School Street in two, that is why we now have School Street West and School Street East.
We are now in School Street East and where it ends here we can see on the right..........

..................Roseville Methodist Chapel.   53.

Coseley Ladies Circle meet in the chapel assembly room on the first and third Thursday's of every month. On April 9th, 1993 they held a Bring and Buy Sale and Coffee Morning.

54.

Left to right - Mrs. Beryl Hunt (nee Dudley), Mrs. Jean Adey (nee Wolverson), Mrs. Brenda Whitehouse (nee Meredith) and Mrs. Joan Allen (nee Chamberlain).

55.

Mrs. Violet Clazey and Mrs. Ida Burgess

56.

57.

Mrs. Sheila Fellows cutting the cake at the second birthday celebrations of the Coseley Ladies Circle. 5th May, 1994.

Miss Irene Turley

20

It was just on the left here, on the corner opposite Roseville Chapel, where School Street East joins Green Street that Coseley council house stood. It was a very smart looking building in red brick with brick letters above stating COSELEY COUNCIL HOUSE. It was built in 1896. The first stone was laid by Richard Clayton who became the first Chairman of Coseley Council.

58.

At one time Coseley was part of Sedgley but they were completely separated in 1867. Coseley was the second largest Urban District in the country and stretched from Parkfield Road on the Wolverhampton border in the north to the far side of the bridge by The British Federal by the Black Country Museum in the south: from Sedgley in the west to Tipton, Wednesbury and Bilston in the east. On the 1st April, 1966, Coseley ceased to be an Urban District and for administration purposes was split up between Dudley, Wolverhampton and West Bromwich (Sandwell). The Council House was demolished in 1968.

If Coseley existed today with its original boundaries it has been estimated that the population would be well over 44,000.

Very close to the Council House in Green Street were several houses and Coseley Fire Station and by the way...

......an unusual house stood here where the chapel car park is today.

59.

60.

We can turn right and walk on the footpath then cross over the top of Bayer Street as we are going to walk now along Avenue Road past Hyde's shop and Coseley Conservative Club. On the opposite corner where the grass is now and the Post Office used to be there was next door to it Wilfred Grainger's corn shop. This place had a smell all its own. This is the shop to where Mr. Jordon moved from Ebenezer Street. Later the shop belonged to Mr. Major Swinnerton then to Mr. Grainger.

61.

62.

The corn shop, Avenue Road.

Coseley Conservative Club adjacent to Hyde's double fronted shop.

Next to the Conservative Club there used to be three houses. The first one was the home of the Gwinnett family. The next one, the other side of the wide entry was where Mr. & Mrs. Blewitt and their daughter Elsie lived. Elsie used to teach shorthand and typing at her home several evenings a week as well as having a full time job as a shorthand typist in a factory office in Tipton. Mr. George Blewitt was a painter and decorator. The third house belonged to Mr. & Mrs. Turner.

63.

64.

The three houses in Avenue Road between the Conservative Club and the Police Station.

Miss Elsie Myra Blewitt born 8th June, 1903 died 18th May, 1983.

The Police Station was next to Mr. & Mrs. Turner's then next to that the Painter's Arms and the house where Mr. & Mrs. Owen used to live.

66.

65.

The Police Station and next door to it....   ......The Painter's Arms

The Police Station was demolished along with the three houses in 1975.   It's good the Painter's Arms and the house next door are still standing.

67.

68.

The land where the Police Station used to stand and the new doctor's surgery is to be built in the not too distant future.

Over the road is number 44 Avenue Road, a large house which for many years has been the Red Cross Centre.

69.

The Red Cross Centre

70.

The next building after the old house by the Painter's Arms is "Alpha House". There was a doctor here at the time of the 1871 census and so there has been ever since. This will be redundant as a doctor's surgery before long.

"Alpha House"

Over the road on the left in its own grounds is Coseley Hall where the Clayton family lived. You can see that the Hall has seen better days although it has recently been smartened with new gates.

71.

Coseley Hall

72.

This is where Avenue Road becomes Old Meeting Road but before we continue along the road which is in fact a railway bridge, can you see over the right towards Wallbrook? There used to be some houses in Railway Terrace which is the path that goes down the other side of the railway line.

Now we are over the other side of the bridge and this is Old Meeting Road. We can see down Railway Terrace where the houses used to be. There were eight of them. The building on the right is Coseley Youth Club, opened by Cllr. Harty in May 1969. Next we come to Old Meeting Unitarian Chapel opposite which is Coseley Library.

The foundation stone of Old Meeting chapel was laid by Charles Cochrane, Esq. on the 16th November, 1874.
This building replaced the earlier one built in 1717.

73.

Old Meeting Chapel

74.

Built within the grounds of Clayton Playing Fields at the outbreak of the 1939-1945 war as a Day Nursery to accommodate children whose mothers were employed in war work. When no longer needed for that reason it became Coseley Library. There used to be twenty-five trees on this side of the road ending at the same point as the railings: now there are eleven.

Carry on along the footpath, around the bend in the road, and where the block of flats is there used to be an Off-licence and some houses. The flats were built in 1972.

75.

Continue around the curve of the road and we shall see Wallbrook House. This is a Home for the elderly and was opened on the 15th April, 1970. Before Wallbrook House occupied this space there was a factory here called The Coseley Welding Company and it was owned by Wallace (Wal) and Harry Hyde. Prior to it being Coseley Welding, Wal Hyde Brothers, Haulage Contractors, was based here. Wal and his brother Harry gave up the haulage business when transport was taken over by the Government not long after the outbreak of the 1939-1945 war.

76.

Wallbrook House in Whitehouse Street.

We'll walk up to the top of Old Meeting Road into Mamble Square so we can see the swimming baths. There used to be a big old house here belonging to a family named Owen. They used to sell petrol from a single pump near the footpath. Where the car park is at the back of the baths was Square Street. This was all demolished about 1960. Coseley Baths was opened on 25th August, 1962 by Cllr. J.T. Wilson.

77.

Coseley Swimming Baths.

26

Let's turn right here and walk into Wallbrook. It's only a short distance to the top of Broad Street. On the right there is St. Cuthbert's Mission, often called the Church Army although there has been no Church Army Captain there since Captain Budden died on 10th December, 1986. He was here for more than fifty years. St. Cuthbert's is a mission church under the supervision of Christ Church which we will see later. At the Wallbrook end of Central Drive there is Budden Road which was named after the Captain in recognition of all that he did for Coseley and its people. The foundation stones which were laid on either side of the porch, one by Joseph Hipkins and the other by Mrs. W.H. Hawthorne are both dated 23rd. June, 1896.

78.

St. Cuthbert's Mission Church.

Just a little farther along Wallbrook Street on our right we can see the Methodist Chapel. This was built to replace the old one which suitably stood in Chapel Street and was demolished along with the rest of Wallbrook in 1956/7 after which time the congregation worshipped in an Army type hut until the new chapel was ready for use. In fact the hut was the very one that stood in School Street where the Summer House pub used to be. It was eventually burned down.

79.

Wallbrook Methodist Chapel, Chapel Street, demolished 1956.

80.

Wallbrook Methodist Chapel, Wallbrook Street.
Foundation stone laid by Sir Harry Spencer 27th April, 1963.

Harry Francis Spencer was born in Coseley on 8th April, 1892. His home was in Sheldon's Terrace off Fullwood's End. In 1916 he married Ethel May Southall the daughter of Cllr. Southall who at one time lived in Old End House where the Clifton Cinema was and Midital is now. Southall Crescent was named after Cllr. Southall. Harry Spencer was knighted in 1963 for his services to the steel industry. He died in London on 31st May, 1964. He is buried in a double grave along with his wife and her parents in Old Meeting grave yard. Cll.r Southall was born 8th September, 1867 and died 27th July, 1927. Lady Ethel May Spencer was born 19th November, 1892 and died 11th April, 1971. The epitaph on the grave stone to Sir Harry Francis Spencer reads - *"Steel true, blade straight"*.

82.

We'll go back into Mamble Square and down Old Meeting Road where the Unitarian Minister's house, the Manse, used to be on the right, then through the Clayton Playing Fields.

The Clayton Playing Fields were presented to the people of Coseley by the family of Alderman Richard Clayton, J.P., after his death. The Playing Fields were opened by his son, R.D.B. Clayton, Esq., of Hardwick Manor, Tewkesbury on 4th May, 1935. The field in the middle has been turned into two football pitches. The ground on the east and west side of the football pitches used to have slides, swings, turntables and other things on which the children could play. In fact on what we called 'the little side' where the smaller children played there was a sandpit. There are a few trees missing now. Just look over to the right. There was a tree across there blown down in a gale.

The tree blown down in the gale
Sunday, 13th March, 1994.

Through the gate on the opposite corner and just down the path we are now facing the entrance to Coseley Railway Station. This is the side where we could catch the train to Birmingham; but not today.

81.

Coseley Railway Station from the bridge in Gough Road.

We are now on the bridge in Gough Road. Gough Road was straightened in 1982 as the bridge was difficult for traffic to negotiate and there was no footpath except for the separate one which had been built in about the late 1950's.

83.

84.

The old bridge in winter looking towards Fullwood's End. The semi-circular construction on the left supported the footbridge.

Taken from Fullwood's End during the mammoth task of the station bridge reconstruction in 1982. Note the bus coming up Gough Road.

85.

Coseley Station, Christmas Day 1961.

86.

Coseley Station, October 1994.

Over the road here in Fullwood's End is a row of three shops.

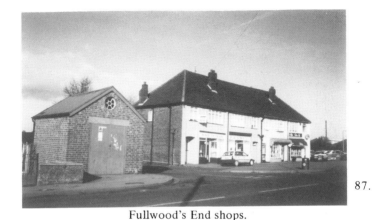

87.

Fullwood's End shops.

Carry on through Fullwood's End to Tunnel Street.   Just where Ivy House Lane is on the right used to be Sheldon's Terrace to the left.   That's where Harry Spencer lived when he was a boy.   There was a house on the corner of Sheldon's Terrace with Tunnel Street where Mr. & Mrs. Gutteridge and their daughters Ethel and Dorothy lived.

88.

Miss Ethel Gutteridge in 1992.

Half way up Tunnel Street on the left where there used to be some houses lying well back from the road now stands Roseville Day Centre. It was opened on the 14th June, 1976 by the Mayor of Dudley, Cllr. Denis Harty. Many retired Coseley residents make use of this place which has wonderful facilities. The old tree outside the Day Centre has grown again beautifully since being severely lopped about 1985, don't you think?

89.   The Roseville Day Centre, 1985........   .....and again in July, 1994.   90.

30

Miss Mildred York, later Mrs. Mildred Holt, used to live in a house on the site of Roseville Day Centre. She died on 22nd January, 1985.

Three houses called "Fern Cottages" and the newsagents along with the house attached to it which were here in 1983 have gone now.

We will turn around and walk back down Tunnel Street by the bungalows and flats on the left.

Ray Elwell who has always been connected with Tunnel Street died in May 1993.

Turn left here into Ivy House Lane. Over on the opposite corner we can see the building which was Kate Gutteridge's shop is still there next to the Horse & Jockey which replaced the pub of the same name. The 'R' and 'E' are missing from the front of the pub. That makes it real Black Country spelling. Oh dear! The '&' is missing as well!

91.

The Horse & Jockey and the old shop.

The present day Horse & Jockey stands behind where the old one was and the business was transferred from one to the other in March 1940. It is nothing short of a miracle that it is still standing because at 9.30 on the night of the 30th August, 1940, the people of Coseley were experiencing an enemy air raid and a bomb hit the Horse & Jockey. The timber in the new roof was excessively strong being pitch pine and the bomb exploded into the atmosphere. Had this not have been so, the licencee, Mr. Bishton, his wife and daughter Patricia and their customers would without doubt all have been killed.

Over the far side of the canal we can see Coseley Secondary School. It was opened by the Minister of Education, Edward Short, M.P., on the 22nd November, 1969.

92.

The Coseley School

It was beautiful weather on the morning I met Mrs. Winchurch and Mr. & Mrs. Cooper here.

93.

Left to right - Edna Cooper, Arthur Cooper and Alice Winchurch
Saturday, 9th July, 1994.

Let's cross over the Birmingham New Road and go up Ivy House Lane and I'll show you how Mount Pleasant School has changed. The Junior School and the Cookery Centre were demolished in January, 1991 and now there are houses on the site. I'm pleased to say that the Senior School is still standing. Look! You can see it through the houses.

94.

Although no longer used as a school it is still a place of learning. Now it is the Local Studies and Archives Centre. Their premises used to be on the top floor of Dudley Library in St. James's Road. There wasn't much room there and moving to here has made researching so much easier. Not only do people come here from all over the country but from all over the world. It opened for this purpose on 30th March, 1992.

95.

Mount Pleasant Local Studies and Archives Centre.

96.

The Archivist, Mrs. Atkins and her Staff.
Left to right - Mrs. K.H. Atkins, Mrs. Jane Humphrey, Mrs. Susan Bell,
Mrs. Diane Matthews, Mr Paul Bowen, Mr. Andrew Bytheway and Mrs. Alison Soars.

Do you remember what it looked like when the Junior School was here? There was ....

97.

Corner of Ivy House Lane and Mount
Pleasant Street with Cookery Centre
extreme left and Junior School right.

98.

Senior School in front, Junior School
and Cookery Centre right, from Ivy
House Lane.

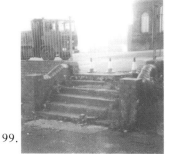

99.

Steps from the playground up to
the terrace.

100.

Caretakers House in Mount
Pleasant Street.

Mr. Stan Grange who used to be Head Master here died in 1985 shortly after the death
of his wife Linda. Mrs. Olive Caddick, better known to most as Miss Stant, and Miss
Sneyd have also died recently.

We'll go back down Ivy House Lane. Here is the pretty cottage which has been here for close on two hundred years. Miss Susan Jeavons lived here years ago but Mr. & Mrs. Westwood live here now.

101.   "Ivy House Cottage", 30th April, 1994.

102.

Go back over the Birmingham New Road. That's the corner where the Ivy House pub used to be.
It was demolished between 7.30 a.m. and 8.30 a.m. on Sunday, 1st November, 1992.

103.

The Ivy House Inn

Mr. & Mrs. C.W. Legge.

The garage on the opposite corner used to be owned by Cal Legge. He, his wife and daughter lived in a detatched house named "Wellington". The house was demolished when the garage changed hands and so was the garage. This one has been built in very recent years.

Carry on down the road past the entrance to the Working Men's Club and its car park where Morgan's Drive used to be up there on the right, with its little houses and past the newer houses to where the little drive leads up to the big house which used to be the home of Nurse Stewart before it was the Food Office during the war. She used to make an ointment to her own formula. I've been told by someone who no longer lives in Coseley that when he was a little boy his mother would take him with her to buy the ointment. It was made there on the premises; golden in colour and put into silver coloured tins of varying sizes. It was known as FMS Ointment - her initials. She was Florence Marion Stewart. No one knows how it was made. She took the formula with her to the grave.

Back now past the Horse & Jockey and into Fullwood's End.
On the left is Kenelm Road. I was told recently that St. Kenelm was a boy King of Mercia and he was martyred on Clent Hills in 821. A holy water spring marks the spot where his body was found and it has been a place of pilgrimage ever since. It is very near to St. Kenelm's Church at Romsley.

104

Kelemn Road.

Over the road, opposite the shops on our left which we saw earlier, there used to be some houses. The front doors opened onto the footpath. There used to be a wall before you came to the houses. It was the boundary wall to Coseley Hall. That's why the cul-de-sac which is there now is called Hall Grove. Where the detatched house called "Trelowth" is, that's the one nearest the railway, there used to be some double gates. This was the back entrance to Coseley Hall. Mr. Brookes who was a chimney sweep lived in one of the old houses and he is well remembered by a good many people.

105.

Fullwood's End in the mid 1950's.

If you didn't ever see Gough Road before the bridge was altered it is difficult to imagine what it was like, but if the old bridge was still there we would have to turn right onto the bridge and then left when on the other side instead of walking straight on as we can do now.

When we crossed over the bridge to where we are now we could see the shops right in front of us. Can you see what I mean?

106. The footbridge over the railway parallel to the station bridge, 107.
Gough Road before 1982.

You can see where it was because today, what was the main road is now a service road for the houses near to the Clayton Playing Fields. Painted on the road are the words KEEP CLEAR.

108.

Where Gough Road bridge was until 1982.

36

Now we'll walk down Gough Road by where the newest houses are now on what was the open land near to...............

109.

110.

111.

........Miss Dolly Millard's house. She died in July 1981 and the house was demolished in September of the same year. It is known that at one time the house was Coseley Police Station.

The people of Coseley couldn't believe the news that The Cannon was to close but it did, officially on 31st March, 1994. The Cannon commenced business in Coseley in 1826 and became famous for gas appliances, cookers and fires etc.. The original factory was at the far end of Havacre Lane and we'll go down there later.

112.

The "Cannon" Offices, Gough Road, built in 1935.

The Mary Dermott Waddell Memorial Hall is still here. It's the Hall which belongs to Christ Church. The Hall is used for many activities including being used twice a year as a blood donor station. The building was given by Dr. Charles Hope Waddell of "Alpha House", Avenue Road, in memory of his mother - Mary Dermott Waddell. Dr. Waddell and his brother, Alex J. Waddell both laid foundation stones on 28th July, 1933, one on either side of the front of the building. Dr. Wadell was born 8th November, 1878 and died on the 21st October, 1953. He is buried in Christ Church grave yard.

Next we come to some houses on the same side of the road and they were built in what was known as Baker's field. There used to be horses kept here.

Carry on now past the church yard wall near to the cross roads. Just stop and look at Christ Church Nursery School. The "Mr. Men" were painted all along the wall of the school by work experience students. Didn't they do well?

113.

Christ Church Nursery School

Turn right into Church Road past the grassed part on the left where there used to be some houses. The nearest one to the school was Dr. Chand's surgery and was called "Mornington House". In 1833 Lord Dudley's executors gave permission for the building of a school and a house for the Master or Mistress on the opposite side of the road from the church. The house was incorporated in the same building and was on the left of the school. It was opened in February, 1834 to children who had been recommended by subscribers "and brought by their parents and friends".

The original Christ Church School used to stand on the ground in front of where the new school is today.

114.

The old Christ Church School in Church Road.

38

The present day Christ Church School is very different from the original school. Pupils first attended this school in September 1972 but it was officially opened by the Lord Bishop of Lichfield, The Right Reverend Arthur Street Reeve, D.D., on the 9th March, 1973.

115.

In 1928 Mr. Joseph (Joby) Webb left his teaching job at Mount Pleasant to become Headmaster of Christ Church School where he remained until his retirement in 1958.
He was loved by all of his pupils and known to them as "Daddy Webb".

116.

Mr. Joseph Webb, died 1978.

Opposite Christ Church School is Christ Church. Let's pause here and look at the Calvary Cross which is the 1914-1918 War Memorial. One of the noble names on it is that of Pte. Tom Barratt, V.C.. In 1987 Mrs. Edna Cox visited his grave in Belgium and took some roses from her garden in Coseley to place there so that he could have some flowers from home. He is buried with his comrades of the South Staffordshire Regiment and his head stone has the V.C. engraved upon it.

117.

118.

The 1914-1918 War Memorial
Christ Church, Coseley.

The grave of Pte. Tom Barratt, V.C.
in Essex Farm Cemetary, Belgium.
2nd Sept., 1987 with roses from Coseley.

119.

120.

The new Vicarage replaced.....................................the old one in the late 1970's and was built before the old one was demolished. The builder named Bradford nailed his name board to the big tree. The tree became dangerous and was cut down in 1980.

The next building we come to in Church Road is the Vicarage. This was built after 1970. The original Vicarage was a very nice looking house with a huge garden which was enclosed behind a high wall which went up the road to where Church Road and The Paddock meet. There it turned the corner going up The Paddock to where it joined the Vicarage back garden. What was the back garden wall of the Vicarage can still be seen today between numbers 69 and 70 The Paddock. The four houses past the Vicarage and the first five in The Paddock are all built on ground which was the Vicarage Garden.

In 1832 there was a cholera epidemic and all who died of this had their names marked with a "C" in the Burial Register. The first one to be marked thus was Thomas Hollis of The Paddock - 5th July, 1832 - age 53. There are 33 other burials marked in this way. The last body to be interred in Christ Church burial ground was that of a small child. Francis Armstrong of Broad Lanes - 6th October, 1832 - age 3 months.

This was before Mr. & Mrs. Thomas Newton and their children lived on The Paddock at number 3, a little house which backed onto the Vicarage wall. There was a pool around here at that time.

121.

Mrs. Hannah Bullock Newton

123.

Mr Thomas Newton

Mrs. Newton was killed by a fall in the house on 19th September, 1899 and it was reported in the paper.

FATAL FALL — Hannah Newton, aged 68, of 30, New Row, Paddock, Coseley, was in the house alone on Monday afternoon, when she met her death in a shocking manner. It appears that the deceased had been suffering from severe headaches for some time, and on Monday seemed worse. She was found shortly after three o'clock lying at the bottom of the cellar steps, with bruises all over her face and a cut on her head. The coals were kept down the cellar, and it is thought that when the deceased was going to fetch some she accidentally fell down.

122.

41

Walk beyond the end of Southall Crescent to where The Paddock divides. Here on the corner is a new house.

124.

New House in The Paddock

Mr. & Mrs. Williams who used to live at "Roseleigh", number 36 would have a surprise if they could see it now.
Jim Williams was born 6th October, 1886 and died 17th November, 1977.
Emily Williams was born 8th September, 1902 and died 29th September, 1968.

125.

Mr. Jim Williams with his wife Emily (formerly Hyde, nee Newton)

Farther up on the left used to live Roderick Hingley before he was ordained to the Priesthood. He is the grandson of the late Noah Hingley who lived in Bayer Street. His mother's father was Mr. Bishton, the licencee of the Horse & Jockey as the time of the air raid.

126.

The Reverend Roderick S.P. Hingley with his mother,
Ordination Day, Sunday, 27th June, 1976 at Lichfield Cathedral.

We'll carry on now towards the path which years ago was known as The Uplands but now the houses are numbered in with The Paddock.

127.

Taken in 1961 outside 50, The Paddock long before 48 and 49 were built.

128.

129.

Mr. Harold Fones, the violin teacher, with his wife Audrey taken 11th April, 1987. Mr Fones died on 15th November, 1993. He was 92.

Here is Glyn Cox on his milk round. He has been delivering milk to this area for over twenty-three years.

Turn around here and we'll walk back to Church Road.

130.

The Paddock looking east.

Just at the back of where these houses are on the left there used to be two houses on a lower level than the ones we can see today. This road was on a level with their bedroom floor. They were the last of the very old houses left in The Paddock and were demolished in the 1950's. Instead of facing south as to-days houses, the front of the old ones looked towards Church Road.

131.   132.

The Paddock in 1994...................................the old houses about the same spot
in the 1950's awaiting demolition.

Walk on down The Paddock towards Church Road.

The Paddock looking towards Church Road.   133.

44

Back at the bottom of The Paddock turn right into Church Road. Make sure to look left as Church Road is now 'one way only' traffic. This house here which is newer than the others stands where the Spread Eagle pub used to be. It was converted into two flats before it was demolished and this house was built.
I'll tell you more about that later.
Here at the end of Church Road where it meets Philip Street is a house which used to be Church Road Post Office. It has now been rough-cast and converted into two flats. It would need a well peeled eye to see where the letter box used to be set in the wall between the window and the door. The Post Office business was transferred to Yew Tree Lane but is still called Church Road Post Office for convenience sake.
We'll see it later on. Mrs. Edna Underhill who was post mistress here died on 12th July, 1986. Prior to Edna being post mistress that job had belonged to her mother, Mrs. Griffiths.

134.

Edna Underhill (left) with her sister-in-law Gwen Griffiths

Before we go over the brow of the hill and down Pemberton Road just look over the other side of the road at the cricket field wall and you'll wonder why some of the bricks don't match. It's because there was a gale on Monday, 26th February, 1990 and the rebuilding repairs were done three months later on 25th May. It must have been impossible to get big cinders to match the original wall. Coseley Cricket Club was established in 1870.

135.

Coseley Cricket Field

136.

137.

The houses in Bradley's Lane which were on the land where Perivale Court is today.

Carry on walking down Bradley's Lane and soon we'll see on the left the drive that leads down to Wallbrook School. The Acting Headmaster, Mr. Dent, told me it was built about 1952. The school is not actually in Wallbrook but was built to accommodate, in the main, children who come from there. The new Headmaster is Mr. Michael Ullah.

138.

Wallbrook School.

As we walk up the drive from the school we can see Brunel Court across the road. Those bungalows there now cover the ground where the semi-detatched cottages stood when the land mine was dropped during the war. They were lived in by Mr. & Mrs. Arthur Smith and Mr. & Mrs. Charles Smith. Arthur and Charles were brothers.

Because of the bomb damage Mr. & Mrs. Arthur Smith went to live with their daughter and son-in-law and family. More of that in a few minutes. Turn left and we'll walk towards Princes End. The railway bridge is still here but the railway has gone along with Princes End Station. This is one of the lines that had "the chop" in the Dr. Beeching railway slaughter, but that's another story. There are some big gates here which used to be the entrance to the sports ground of W.G. Allen Ltd., an old firm which closed about March 1985. There is a sign here which tells us we are now in Sandwell, in other words West Bromwich but we'll ignore that at the moment. There are two houses on the left then just beyond there used to be a row of small houses coming right onto the footpath. One of them used to be a fish and chip shop which was owned by Trevor Charnell who used to live at "The Warren", Bayer Street before he married Pam, the daughter of Noah Hingley. On our right is the Railway Inn then a few yards farther on is the Talbot Inn which is on the corner of Fountain Lane. If we walk to the traffic lights we'll cross over where Bloomfield Road and Princes End High Street meet. That will bring us onto the corner of Newhall Street.

The boundary between Coseley and Tipton ran down the middle of Princes End High Street so we are now on the Tipton side. Behind us is The Royal, an old pub, and across the road on the corner of Bradley's Lane and Bloomfield Road is a one storey building which is now referred to as The Scratching Factory. Some years ago it was a two storey building and was the Prince of Wales pub. On the opposite corner where the advertising hoardings are now was W.G. Allen's factory. The offices and the gates were the last of it to be demolished. Lots of people were put out of work when Allens closed.

They were manufacturers of industrial boilers.

139.

W.G. Allen Ltd., corner of Bradley's Lane and High Street, Princes End.

We'll walk down High Street now and just here on the right where there are some new houses there used to be an unusual pair of semi-detatched houses. The second one was owned by Mr. & Mrs. Gill and they lived there with their children Dorothy and Geoffrey. Mrs. Gill was the daughter of Mr. & Mrs. Arthur Smith who had to move from their cottage in Bradley's Lane after the land mine fell there and this was where they came to live. Mr. & Mrs. Gill were both very well known not only by Tipton people but by many who lived in Coseley as they were both piano teachers. Mr. William Abraham Gill died on 1st May, 1983.

140.

Mr. Wm. A. Gill., F.R.C.C., C.H.M., F.T.C.L., L.R.A.M., A.B.S.M. and Mrs. Ethel M. Gill., L.R.A.M., A.R.C.M., L.T.C.L.

A bit farther down on the same side lived another well known Tipton person who also had connections with residents of Coseley.

Sam Morgan was a coal merchant and he delivered coal all over the area.

Mr. Morgan now lives with his son John and daughter-in-law Doreen at their home "Blakelands" at Halfpenny Green. (Ha' penny Green). Not only a beautiful 18th century house but a first class restaurant because premises at the rear of the house have been converted for this purpose.

141.

Mr. Sam Morgan (left) in the grounds of "Blakelands" on 20th May, 1992, with Mr. & Mrs. Arthur Gorin on holiday from Jersey.

Mr. & Mrs. Gorin very much enjoy holidays in the Black Country.
Betty is a Tipton lady; Arthur is a Jersey man.

You must have heard about the Crooked House at Himley! Well over the road, on the Coseley side where the corner of Parkes Lane meets High Street you can see our very own crooked house. It's called the Tilted Barrel. Crooked for the same reason as the one at Himley: mining subsidence.

142.

The Tilted Barrel, 24th July, 1994

Farther down the High Street on the left is a small housing estate built by Coseley Council. Most of the roads were named after members of Coseley Council. Proof, if proof were needed, that this part of Princes End came under the jurisdiction of Coseley Urban District Council.

We'll go back up to the traffic lights and turn right into Bradley's Lane. On the left is Minith Road. The original houses there were built by Mr. Clifford Hipkins. He was always known as "Digger" but I don't know why. It was he who named the road Minith Road after a place called Minith Wood near to Stockton-on-Teme because he and his wife and family used to go to stay with friends who lived there.
The next road on the left is Dimmocks Avenue. Mr. Hipkins also built these houses. The Avenue is named after people named Dimmock with whom the Hipkins family used to stay in Blackpool. Both roads were built in the 1930's.

Bear right here in Summerhill Road. On the right are three new houses which have replaced the pair of semis owned by Christopher Cox. His shop was on the right side and he lived in the one on the left. Mr. Cox died in August, 1989.

We'll carry on up Summerhill Road to the brow of the hill and on the other side of the road we can see the Sherlock Holm pub. That's the place which was "Albert House" before it had its name changed to the Spread Eagle when the business was transferred from Church Road.

143.

The Sherlock Holmes, 1994

48

Oh! I know what I want to show you: Brierley Lane. It's to the right at the bottom of Harding Street. When the railway was put through from Bilston to Dudley there was a bridge put over the line here. The trains used to run under this bridge and along the line to the railway station at the bottom of Bradley's Lane where I showed you a while ago. In recent years traffic lights were put up to make it safer as the bridge was narrow but in January this year demolition of the bridge was started.
Now the bridge and the traffic lights have gone.
The pretty house on the left used to be a pub called the Bricklayer's Arms but it hasn't been a pub for a long time.

144.

The bridge in Brierley Lane

145.

Brierley Lane without the bridge.

49

It we turn around and cross over into Skidmore Road I'll show you Adams's Garage. I've been told it's going to be demolished so we'd better look at it now.

146.

Adams's Garage, Skidmore Road

We'll turn around and walk back to the cross roads. Stay on this side of the road and we'll walk up Harding Street then turn right into Yew Tree Lane. There is a telephone kiosk over the road which hasn't been there very long. That's the area where the old Georgian house called "Chez Nous" used to stand. Mr. William Mason Akerman lived there. He was a Solicitor and Commissioner for Oaths and the brass plate on the front door stated this. "Chez Nous" was demolished in the 1940's. It faced onto Summerhill Road and where its back garden was there now stands a very nice new bungalow.

147.

New bungalow and view of Yew Tree Lane.

Opposite the bungalow, here on our right, is the Roman Catholic Church of St. John Fisher. By kind permission of Father Casey the church is also used by the community of St. Cedd who are hoping to be received into the Antiochian Orthodox Church under the care of the Patriarch of Antioch later this year.
St. Cedd was St. Chad's brother and was the first evangelist of the Midlands.

148.

The Roman Catholic Church of St. John Fisher
Consecrated on 22nd September, 1960 by Archbishop Gimshaw

149.

150.

Father Philip Casey, 1994   Father Kurt Wittwer, 1994

At the top of Yew Tree Lane on this side are three shops. The first is an Off-licence, the second belongs to Geoff Ward, the butcher and the third is Church Road Post Office which I explained about when we were in Church Road.

151.

Shops in Yew Tree Lane

152.

Mr. Geoffrey Ward

We are now on the cross roads where Yew Tree Lane, Church Road, Gough Road and Legge Lane meet. It is difficult to believe but there used to be several houses on this grassed triangle of land.

153.

The cross roads looking towards Gough Road with Christ Church Nursery School playground on the left. More "Mr. Men"!

Turn right and we'll walk along Legge Lane and bear left up the incline at the end of the road. There is a cross roads here. The left turn is Webb Street but we'll turn right into Bell Street. We'll go and look at Highfields Primary School and say "Hello" to the Headmaster, Mr. Woodhall. He's been here for five years and before that he was at Christ Church Primary School for nearly fourteen years. He's very clever at writing music for the school plays and pantomimes.
Before Mr. Woodhall came to Highfields, Mr. Ian Roberts was Headmaster.

Highfields Primary School
officially opened on 29th September, 1972 by Cllr. J.T. Wilson

Mr. Paul Woodhall

Back now at the top of Bell Street we'll turn right. We are now by Darkhouse Baptist Chapel. On the 22nd May, 1915 the marriage took place between................

156.

.........Mr. Walter Edwards of Birmingham and Miss Hannah Thomas of Coseley. Their photograph was taken in the grounds at the back of the chapel.

We can't go past Darkhouse without mentioning Harry Hughes who was connected all of his life with this chapel.
He was not only organist and President of the Girl's and Boy's Brigade but he did dozens of other things besides.
Harry was also well known by all who had worked at The Cannon because for years he was the foundry manager.
Harry died on 3rd November, 1993. He was 75.

Darkhouse Chapel was built in 1785. It has recently been realised that it is not a viable proposition to carry out structural repairs so the chapel is soon to be demolished and a new one built on nearby chapel land.

157.

With his wife Gladys is Harry, proudly wearing his R.A.F. tie.

Next to Darkhouse Chapel is an old building. It's a factory called Halesowen Fastenings. They make things such as nuts and bolts. This place used to be Repairwell - the dry cleaners. This was where the dry cleaning was done. Remember we saw in Roseville where one of their shops used to be?
Next to this place is the pub called the Rising Sun.
Walk down Darkhouse Lane and around the bend to the right. On the land on the left there used to be a row of thirteen terraced houses.
Here we go under the railway bridge.

We are now in Havacre Lane. It looks much different now since The Cannon stack was taken down and Bridgewater Estate was built on the site in 1984.

158.

159.

The Cannon stack..........

and all that was left of the 'old side' of The Cannon before Bridgewater Estate was built in 1984.

Past where The Cannon wall used to be there are still two quaint cottages.

160.

Cottages in Havacre Lane.

I must show you where the big old house used to be on the corner where the path goes down to the bottom of Kenelm Road.
This is where 31 and 32 are now: 33 is where the back garden of the old house was.

The old house faced up Havacre Lane. There were two very old cottages which looked out toward the side of the old house.

161.

Two elderly ladies lived in the tiny cottages which was 35, Havacre Lane.
They were Mrs. Elizabeth (Bet) Price and her sister Miss Mary (Polly) Newton.
Coseley born and bred, Mrs. Price spent several years of her life nursing in the U.S.A.
Miss Newton came back to Coseley after spending her life in Service to a Deaconess in Gateshead-on-Tyne.
They are both buried in Darkhouse graveyard.
When we were in The Paddock I told you about their mother and father.

162.

Mrs. Elizabeth Price (1865-1943)
on the left and
Miss Mary Newton(1859-1935)

163.

The cottages, 35 and 36 Havacre Lane, didn't have any gas or electricity: only oil lamps. Number 35 was the smallest one and was next door to the house which is still standing today. There was only one living room where all the cooking was done in the oven of the firegrate. This was called a range. There was only one bedroom. To get to the wash-house where the only water tap was, one had to go outside down a narrow passage. Next to the wash-house was the toilet.
The railway line, as you can imagine, was very near.

164.

You can see what the same spot looks like today.

We will turn and walk down to the bottom of Havacre Lane. Opposite the Boat Inn is where the railway station used to be. It was transferred to its present position sometime between the 11th October, 1899 and the 31st May, 1902 as the Coseley men who fought in the Boer War left from the old station and the survivors came back to the new one.

Go round the corner by the old post office. We are now in Biddings Lane and behind the road name plate on the wall we can still see where the letter box used to be.

These premises are now called Cob's Corner: in other words a sandwich shop. At one time it did have a sign on it saying The Boat. It has been Cob's Corner since 1989.

165.
The old post office now Cob's Corner.

166.
The canal from Biddings Lane bridge.

We'll stop here on the canal bridge and look towards the tunnel which comes out at the bottom of Ivy House Lane by the Horse & Jockey. Have a rest while I tell you about it.

The earliest reference to a canal through Coseley is in the Quarter Sessions records dealing with public undertakings, in the form of a plan dated 1793. In 1794 and 5 an Act of Parliament authorised the cutting of a branch canal to Coseley. This was to extend from Bloomfield to Deepfields. It was not completed until after 1835 when provision was made for further extentions throughout the district. An Act of that year (5William IV,c39) cut a canal "from and out of Birmingham Canal near a Bridge called WALLBROOK BRIDGE to join and communicate with the Birmingham Canal at or near IVY HOUSE LANE". This canal, it is stated in the Act, was intended to complete the "Cut or Communications already begun between Bloomfield and Deepfield. It was to be opened for traffic not later than 25th June 1837. This of course involved the cutting of the Coseley Tunnel and presumably the inordinate length of time taken to complete the Bloomfield - Deepfield's branch was due to this fact. Brindley and Telford were both engaged in the construction of the canal and the task was full of difficulties".*

The tunnel goes at an angle under part of Tunnel Street, directly under where stood the post office in Roseville, under the end of Avenue Road, under the top of Bayer Street and where the OLD Roseville Chapel stood, under School Street (East) and finishes at the bottom of Old End Lane by Garbriel's Wharf.

There used to be a clock and watch repairers shop just here but it was knocked down so the back yard of The Boat is bigger than it was.

*Extract from "The History of Coseley" by J.S. Roper, M.A.

We'll carry on up Biddings Lane past the bungalows on this side of the road. Over the road where Meadow Lane bears round to the right you can see the Post Office which replaced the one on the corner of Havacre Lane. This area of Coseley is called Deepfields. Cross over the end of Hinchliffe Avenue. This is where Biddings Lane becomes Shaw Road. Let's take a deep breath because it's quite a pull up here.

Now we have come to the Birmingham New Road where Fellows's Garage used to be on the right hand side of the road.

167.

168.

Mr. Albert Jeavons (extreme left), Mr. Alan Fellows (second left).

Second from the right in white overalls is Mr. George Fellows who was no relation until he married Alan's daughter Sheila in 1954. Alan was born in 1903 and died in 1976.

There is nothing on this land now and Mr. Fellows's house called "Bowesfield" which was on the end, and the next two houses were demolished so the house on the end was originally the fourth house. There is always a big advertisement on the side of that house.

The Birmingham New Road is always very busy so we must be careful how we cross.

We have now crossed over the Birmingham New Road and we are on the level for a little way. This is still Shaw Road. The White Horse pub is still on the corner of Upper Ettingshall Road. Turn left here because we are going up Upper Ettingshall Road by where Mobberley's Brick Works used to be.

Here on the right is Upper Ettingshall Methodist Chapel. It is known usually as Sodom Chapel because this area of Coseley is known as Sodom.

169.

Upper Ettingshall Methodist Chapel re-built in 1850.

The chapel is on the corner of Paul Street and that's where we are going so turn right here. Before long we will see Hurst Hill Primary School on the left.
This school was opened officially on 2nd March, 1987 by The Rt. Hon. Neil Kinnock, M.P. although it had been in use since November of the year before. The Headmistress is Mrs. Sue Barkway.

170.

Hurst Hill Primary School.

If we carry on up Paul Street we will come out in Can Lane. Well, that's what everybody used to call it before it was re-named Hurst Road. We'll turn left and up there on the right we can see Hurst Hill Methodist Chapel.
There is a memorial stone on the side of it that was laid by David Groucott, Esq., on the 6th June, 1864.

Hurst Hill Methodist Chapel. 171.

172.

The old Post Office at Hurst Hill.

On the corner of Hollywell Street where we have come to now there used to be Hurst Hill Post Office. For many years the Postmistress was Miss Williams. The premises were demolished in 1973.
Council houses now stand on this site. The new Post Office is across the road. It's one of the new shops higher up the road from the chapel.
John Roper wrote in his "History of Coseley", 'There are, of course, many and varied stories of healing wells in this part of Staffordshire, but the tradition in Coseley is that a well dedicated to Lady Wulfruna has been a long one; both Spring Vale and Holywell (at Hurst Hill) claiming to be the site of Wulfruna's healing well'.

This road is very steep but we must look at Dr. Baker's statue, so we'll cross over and walk up the other side of the road. The statue is on the corner of Hall Lane. The bust on the tall plinth was erected by public subscription to the memory of I.J. BAKER, L.R.C..S., L.M., of Hurst Hill.

The inscription on the plinth reads,

"He endeared himself to all who knew him by the uprightness of his charecter, his sympathy with the suffering, and especially by his kindness to the poor. To many in afliction he was a spritiual adviser, and cheered the dying with his prayers and words of comfort. By his good deeds, he being dead yet speaketh".

173.

Dr. Baker's statue.

Let's just go a little farther up towards Sedgley and look at St. Mary's Church. St. Mary's Church Hall, called the Activity Centre, was opened by the Bishop of Lichfield on 6th April, 1975. The church was built in 1873.

174.

St. Mary's Church, Hurst Hill.

Where we are now on the footpath by the Activity Centre is Gorge Road. Up to the right where the road disappears around the bend is known as The Gorge and just out of sight is the Coseley/Sedgley boundary. It's so pretty through The Gorge and the trees almost meet over the road. Cross over the road and walk down to the cross roads and turn right by the Old Gate Inn.

We are now in Clifton Street. Used to be Hurst Hill Street, so I'm told.

Up here on the right is where Len Weaver had his bakery. The bread was super!

175.

On the left side of the road we'll go past the Labour Club. If we look between the houses we'll see a spectacular view over towards Cannock, Walsall, Great Barr and Birmingham. It's quite a sight at night when it's all lit up.

On the right side of the road is Hartland's the undertakers. There aren't any Hartlands in the business now but it's still called by that name.

Instead of becoming an undertaker, David Hartland went into the Priesthood and is now Vicar of St. Stephen's Church, Willenhall. He married Mary Clarke, a Coseley girl on the 18th May, 1959.

Margaret, one of their three daughters married Nicholas Turley on the 5th July, 1986. Her father conducted the ceremony.

The wedding of Margaret Hartland and Nicholas Turley.

Here we are now at the end of Clifton Street. In front of us we can see the side of Hurst Hill Tavern. It faces the fields which are between Coseley and Sedgley. It's such a lovely view, we'll have a look at it before we go any farther.

176.

The road here which goes through to Sedgley is not for traffic, well only up to where the houses end then it becomes a footpath only. This is called Turls Hill Road. The brook we shall see later rises in these hills. I'll tell you more about that later.

177.

Hurst Hill Tavern.

We must turn away from the beautiful view and walk past Hurst Hill Tavern on our right. Over on the left is...............

178.

..............Coppice Baptist Chapel which was built in 1804. The extension at the back was built in 1875. This is Caddick Street.

Come on! We'll go down King Street and into Bourne Street. The Brook Inn is still here on the right but the houses and Woodsetton Works which used to be here have gone now, but there have been some very nice houses and bungalows built on the land. This happened about 1985.

179.

Brook Street today.

Do you remember the old houses that used to be at the top of Brook Street on the left? Well you can still see two of them, but not here!
They were carefully taken down and re-erected in The Black Country Museum.

180.

Brook Street houses in The Black Country Museum.

Turn around and we'll go back the way we came past The Cottage Spring over on the left. Next door to it is Dr. Broad's Surgery.

181.

The Cottage Spring Inn, 8th July, 1994.

Walk along Brook Street, into Bourne Street up the incline and bear right into Bond Street and stop at the cross roads. Over the other side of the road at the opposite end of Upper Ettingshall Road from where we saw the White Horse Inn is Coseley Tavern.

182.

Coseley Tavern.

Keep on this side of the road and bear right into Coppice Road. Just a little way along on the other side of the road are three detatched houses. Before they were built there stood a mid-18th century house on this site. The house was called "Crowesbridge" and it was number 5 Coppice Road. The Mills family lived there. The house was demolished about 1970.

183.

Miss Mary Mills (now Mrs. Stan Vickers) outisde "Crowesbridge".

184.

New houses being built in Coppice Road, 8th July, 1994.

About ten years ago I was walking down here one day when I saw Mrs. Mercy Parton and Mrs. Winifred Whitehouse who were next door neighbours.
This is the same Mrs. Whitehouse who had the fish and chip shop next door to Mr. Reynold's butchers in Roseville. Mrs. Parton died some time ago but Mrs. Whitehouse only died last year on the 22nd August, 1993 just three weeks before her 94th birthday.

185.

Mrs. Mercy Parton (left) and
Mrs. Winifred Whitehouse.

Down Coppice Road to where it becomes Ivy House Lane and turn right where the Ex-Servicmen's Club is on the corner. Do you remember it when it was Page's Picture House, later called The Cosy Cinema?
Now we are in Providence Row. The road goes up a rise and then levels out. On the left are some of the oldest remaining houses in Coseley. I don't exactly know how old they are but I do think they look nice.

186.

Providence Row, 8th July, 1994.

Go past them now and if you think there is something different about the corner of Hospital Lane here on the right, you are right! The old Providence Baptist Chapel is missing. It was demolished in 1993.

187.

The old Providence Baptist Chapel which was built in 1809
being demolished Friday, 30th April, 1993.

The newer Providence Baptist Chapel which was built in 1870 was originally a two storey building. Around the 1970's it was converted into a one storey building very cleverly without losing its character.

188.

Providence Baptist Chapel built 1870.

Down the road now into Portland Place and on the left is where St. Chad's Day School used to be.

189.

St Chad's School
enduring vandalism prior to demolition.

Miss Turner used to be Headmistress at St. Chad's Day School. She was a friend of Mrs. Bourne, the wife of the Vicar in the 1940's.
Miss Turner died on 20th April, 1983. Mrs. Bourne has also died.

190.

Miss H. Ethel Turner (left) and
Mrs. Margaret Bourne.

Just a little way down the road and we are now at the brow of Mason Street and on the left is the pub called the Hop & Barley Corn. I can remember when Mr. Attwell, who was a Coseley Councillor, was licencee here. The new pub was built before the old one was demolished. That was around the late 1950's.

191.

The old Hop & Barley Corn in its last days with the new one being built at the rear.

During 1989/90 there were some houses built on Coseley Moor. This is the land between where we are standing and St. Chad's Church and The Mill.

192.

Coseley Moor as it was.

193.

Coseley Moor today.

Years ago this immediate area around the Hop & Barley Corn was called Littleworth, hence today's Littleworth Avenue. We'll go now down Chad Road to where the shops are. Do you see here on the left, roughly where Rosalind Avenue comes into Park Road? Do you know that a hundred years ago this area was called The Bull Ring? It is shown on the Ordnance Survey map of 1887. Carry on to the traffic lights by the Bramford School and the Bramford Inn. Bramford School opened on 11th January, 1955. The first Headmaster was Mr. Roger Gowland who died in March 1976. This is where Tipton Road on our right joins Sedgley Road on our left. Cross over here. Now we are in Parkes Hall Road and on our left is the Midlands Electricity Board sub-station. This is just where the brook runs through a duct under the road and the foot-path. We'll pass the pair of semi-detatched houses and the detatched house on the left then turn sharp left. Now we can see Woodsetton Methodist Chapel. It was built in 1882. At the back of the chapel and the Sunday School building is a very heavily wooded area called Mons Hill.

194.

Woodsetton Methodist Chapel.

Now we have walked past the chapel I can show you the brook. Just after here the brook is piped again and stays on this side of the road until it goes under Sedgley Road and between number 122 and where the Toll House used to be. It then flows at the back of the houses, under Vicarage Road West, the back of the flats in Regent Street and under the Birmingham New Road. From there it goes under Bean Road then open course adjoining the Sewage Works at Foxyards. It then passes via a syphon culvert under the Birmingham Canal. It is then alter-nately open and closed until it reaches the railway line under which is passes through a culvert. It then runs under Bloomfield Road, the end of Speed Road, under the corner of Sycamore Road, Central Drive at the junction of Oval Road and Laurel Road then Elm Crescent and the end of Belmont Close.

195.

The brook at Woodsetton.

Here it goes at the back of Central Avenue School and under the traffic lights at the junction of Locarno Road, Powis Avenue and Church Lane. From there it runs at the back of Tipton Cemetary, under Bridge Road and through the culvert alongside the canal under Toll End Road and the back of Reever Road. It then runs through the Sewage Works at the back of the M.E.B. Area Office in Toll End Road and into the River Tame.

It is of interest to note that the River Tame runs through Birmingham passing through Perry Barr and Bromford curving its way to Water Orton, under the A446, alongside the A423 then under the A5 then under the A513 to join the River Trent near Croxall. The River Trent runs through Nottingham and Newark and eventually, along with the River Ouse and several other rivers and canals, flows out to form the River Humber which proves that not only do great oaks grow from little acorns but also mighty rivers from little brooks including the one from Turls Hill, Coseley.

There's a footpath down here which goes up the side of the sub-station and brings us out by the traffic lights. Turn right here and we'll go down into Swan Village.
Over the other side of the road beyond Claycroft Terrace is where the Toll House used to be that I just mentioned when I was telling you about the brook. It was 124 Sedgley Road. It's not there now but I'm pleased to say it's gone to join the Brook Street houses in the Black Country Musuem so you can still see it.

196.

The Toll House photographed in The Black Country Museum.

Here we are now on the cross roads where Vicarage Road West goes left but we are going to look right here up George Street so we can see Edwin (Teddy) Holden's Brewery and The Park Inn.

197.

The Park Inn and Brewery, 1st August, 1994.

As we go towards the Fox Yards traffic lights on the Birmingham New Road we'll come to Mount Tabor Methodist Chapel. It was built in 1859. It is right next to the Summer House pub.

198.

Mount Tabor Methodist Chapel and The Summer House Inn.

199.

Now we have reached the busy Foxyards cross roads. Stop before we cross over the road, because there is something I want to show you just down there, over on the other side of the road where the 'D' shaped piece of ground is which has been railed off, there used to be a shed which amazingly was a cobbler's shop. It was there for many years.

The Cobbler's Shop, Foxyards.
1st October, 1986.

Now we'll cross over, with care of course, and walk a little way down Sedgley Road West. We must look at the painting on the side of the Rag and Mop pub.
The pub has always been known as the Rag and Mop although its official name was the Foxyards Inn. Now the pub has a new landlord and after suggesting to Banks's Brewery that the name should be changed they readily agreed. The painting was done by Gregory Smith and Alan Neachell of Principle Systems Ltd. of Witton, Birmingham. Impressive isn't it?

200

The Rag and Mop, Sedgley Road West.

Turn back now to the cross roads and cross back over the road to where the cobbler's shop was. Turn right and we'll walk past where Carol's Garage used to be. It is now called Hire and Drive. Just here there is a pedestrian underpass. This has been here since the Birmingham New Road was opened in 1927. It's original use was for the cows to get to the field to graze on the other side of the road where the head office of Alcan Metal Centres Ltd. is now.

The cows belonged to someone in Swan Village. Cross over the top of Vicarage Road West. If we turn up Oak Street we can go home through the park but I'll show you what happened to the big old tree by the north-west door of St Chad's Church. It was blown down in a gale on Tuesday, 21st December, 1993.

It really looks different now.

The remains of the old tree by St. Chad's Church with Ken Wilkes counting the rings to try to find out the age.

Father Percy Bourne was Vicar of St. Chad's from 1940 - 1948.

202.

The Reverend Percy Bourne.

73

The Mother's Union at St. Chad's have always had an annual outing and on............

203.

........17th September, 1954 the Mother's Union outing was to the Wedgewood Factory in The Potteries.

Back down Oak Street now and before we go into the park we can see the Church Hall on the right.
Lots of people hire the hall for celebrations and that's what Cllr. Bob Griffiths did when he was made Mayor of Dudley in 1981.
His wife, Jo, was the Mayoress.

204.

The Mayor and Mayoress
cutting the celebration cake
May, 1981.

Now we'll go into the park.

I remember walking here one day when I was a little girl with my friend Mary. We had been to Sunday School and with Father Bourne's permission we had picked bluebells in the Vicarage garden. My mother, brother and cousin had come to meet us bringing with them our Wire-haired Fox Terrier, Spot.

205.

Mary Banks, Beryl Hyde, Mrs. Emily Hyde, John Hyde and
Albert "Bob" Newton and Spot.

"The ceremony of the opening of the Silver Jubilee Park took place on 30th May, 1936 but was sadly interfered with by the wind and rain - the wind was positively arctic. There was, however, a good crowd of people in spite of the unfavourable weather, and a spirit of cheerfulness about the event, which inaugurated, as one of the speakers said, "a new era for Coseley". The new Park should prove to be a great blessing for the people here, and we hope it will be valued and used. The opening day was a great day for Councillor Grange, the Chairman of Coseley Council, who performed the ceremony, and it was most fitting that Councillor Grange who had done so much to secure this beautiful Park for the people of Coseley, should be the one to formally open it".

That's what Father Esau wrote in St. Chad's Magazine in July, 1936.   206.

We are coming to the bowling green on our left and on the far side of that are the tennis courts which have been re-layed this year. Through the trees we can see the Pavillion.

We are now coming to the Park Keepers House where Mr. & Mrs. Balshaw and their son Walter used to live.

During the war Mr. Balshaw and the park gardeners used to grow tomatoes in the greenhouses. The word would go around like a bush telegraph that the tomatoes were ripe and we would queue at the back door of the Park House and down the path out through the park gates just to get a quarter of a pound. (¼lb.).
They were a real treat.

The Bowling Green
on the Silver Jubilee Park.

If we look through the trees to the right and across the Birmingham New Road we can see the house from where we started. Carry on along the path and through the avenue of trees aren't they beautiful?

207.

208.

We are now coming to the Park Keepers House..................

209.

210.

........where Mr. & Mrs. Balshaw and their son Walter used to live.

Out through the gate we'll turn right and you will see that we are nearly home. There is a zebra crossing here and we'll cross over the Birmingham New Road. Over the other side of Grange Park we can see the houses in Vicarage Road. Did you know that Billy Wright who used to be Captain of Wolverhampton Wanderers football team had a connection with Coseley? He did! He used to live across there at number 10, Vicarage Road. He lodged with Mrs. Colley when he went to the Wolves first in 1938. He was captain of Wolves when they won the F.A. Cup in 1949. He finished playing for the team at the end of the 1959/60 season. He married Joy Beverley of the famous singing trio, the Beverley Sisters. Billy died on September 3rd, 1994.

211.

Billy Wright
(Photograph by Bob Wyper, A.C.P.)

When Grange Park was first put here it had a Band Stand and it was decorated with bunting for the Coronation celebreations in May, 1937. The Band Stand was dismantled many years ago and now where the Band Stand was there is a large, grass cross and on every Remembrance Sunday there is a parade which includes members of every local organisation and ex-Service men and women and many members of the community and a memorial service is held here. The grass cross is covered with poppy wreathes and single poppies, the Union Jack is flown at half mast and everybody remembers those who died to save Britain and make it a great place in which to live.

212.

213.

Coronation celebreations, May, 1937.   Remembrance Sunday

Now we are back where we started and Mrs. Rickward is waiting for us.

214.

Mrs. Sarah "Sally" Rickward, 8th July, 1994.

Here we are back home again. I do hope it hasn't been too much for you but what memories we've stirred.

78